D1278452

Cocurricular Activities:
Their Values and Benefits

Academic Societies and Competitions
Striving for Excellence

Career Preparation Clubs
Goal Oriented

Community Service
Lending a Hand

Foreign Language Clubs
Discovering Other Cultures

Hobby Clubs
Sharing Your Interests

Intramural Sports
Joining the Team

School Publications
Adventures in Media

Science and Technology Clubs
Ideas and Inventions

Student Government and Class Activities
Leaders of Tomorrow

Theater, Speech, and Dance
Expressing Your Talents

Vocal and Instrumental Groups
Making Music

Cocurricular Activities:
Their Values and Benefits

Vocal and Instrumental Groups

Making Music

Judy Garty

37268000125328

Mason Crest Publishers
Philadelphia

Mason Crest Publishers, Inc.
370 Reed Road
Broomall, PA 19008
(866) MCP-BOOK (toll free)
www.masoncrest.com

First printing

1 2 3 4 5 6 7 8 9 10

Library of Congress Cataloging-in-Publication Data

Garty, Judy.
    Vocal and instrumental groups: making music/by Judy Garty.
        p. cm. (Cocurricular activities)
    ISBN 1-59084-895-0
1. School music—Instruction and study. 2. Singing—Instruction and study.
3. Instrumental music—Instruction and study. I. Title. MT3.U5G368 2005
    780'.71'2—dc22
        2004015857

Produced by
Choptank Syndicate, Inc. and Chestnut Productions, L.L.C.
260 Upper Moss Hill Road
Russell, Massachusetts 01071

Project Editors Norman Macht and Mary Hull
Design and Production Lisa Hochstein
Picture Research Mary Hull

OPPOSITE TITLE PAGE

Whether instrumental or vocal, music requires lots of practice and time from students, but it also offers great satisfaction.

Table of Contents

Introduction

COCURRICULAR ACTIVITIES BUILD CHARACTER

Sharon L. Ransom
Chief Officer of the Office of Standards-Based Instruction
for Chicago Public Schools

Cocurricular activities provide an assortment of athletic, musical, cultural, dramatic, club, and service activities. They provide opportunities based on different talents and interests for students to find their niche while developing character. Character is who we really are. It's what we say and how we say it, what we think, what we value, and how we conduct ourselves in difficult situations. It is character that often determines our success in life and cocurricular activities play a significant role in the development of character in young men and women.

Cocurricular programs and activities provide opportunities to channel the interests and talents of students into positive efforts for the betterment of themselves and the community as a whole. Students who participate in cocurricular activities are often expected to follow certain rules and regulations that prepare them for challenges as well as opportunities later in life.

Many qualities that build character are often taught and nurtured through participation in cocurricular activities. A student learns to make commitments and stick with them through victories and losses as well as achievements and disappointments. They can also learn to build relationships and work collaboratively with others, set goals, and follow the principles and rules of the discipline, club, activity, or sport in which they participate.

Students who are active in cocurricular activities are often successful in school because the traits and behaviors they learn outside of the classroom are important in acquiring and maintaining their academic success. Students become committed to their studies and set academic goals that lead them to triumph. When they relate behaviors, such as following rules or directions or teaming with others, to the classroom, this can result in improved academic achievement.

Students who participate in cocurricular activities and acquire these character-rich behaviors and traits are not likely to be involved in negative behaviors. Peer pressure and negative influences are not as strong for these students, and they are not likely to be involved with drugs, alcohol, or tobacco use. They also attend school more regularly and are less likely to drop out of school.

Students involved in cocurricular activities often are coached or mentored by successful and ethical adults of good and strong character who serve as role models and assist students in setting their goals for the future. These students are also more likely to graduate from high school and go on to college because of their involvement in cocurricular activities.

In this series you will come to realize the many benefits of cocurricular activities. These activities bring success and benefits to individual students, the school, and the community.

The members of Tone Appétit, an a cappella barbershop quartet, credit their success to an early interest in music and the valuable experience they gained from school musical productions.

1

Tone Appétit

Four Oklahoma high school girls stepped beyond their school musical stage, piano bench, and choir room into the international spotlight by hitting just the right notes together. Drawing on the training and experience they got from their school's musical productions, classmates at Oklahoma City's Classen School of Advanced Studies (SAS)—a performing arts school for grades six through twelve—the girls formed Tone Appétit, an a cappella barbershop quartet. (A capella is a type of singing done without musical accompaniment.)

Tenor Katarina Nortz, seventeen; lead singer Lisa Marie Lopez, seventeen; baritone Sephra Osburn, fourteen; and bass Emerald Lessley, fifteen, also sing as the youngest members of Oklahoma City's City Chorus of Sweet Adelines, which in 2002 ranked in the top ten of Sweet Adeline International (SAI) in Nashville. The quartet's *Tone Appétit: What's Cookin'* CD was runner up in the Contemporary A Capella Recording Award (CARA) competition for best high school album, and the quartet was honored as the first high school barbershop group on the World's Best High School A Capella Compilation CD 2003. The girls placed third in the SAI 2002 Rising Star Contest and second in 2003. Standing ovations from crowds of more than ten thousand greeted them after they performed on SAI Contest stages at Nashville in 2002 and Phoenix in 2003.

Together just over two years, the quartet has created parodies to old barbershop songs like "No One Loves You Any Better Than Your M-O-double M-Y" instead of the original "M-A-double M-Y," "Flirty Guys" instead of "Flirty Eyes," and their tribute to McDonald's Restaurant "We Are Hung-a-ry" instead of "We Are Family." Their costumes include checkered aprons and chef hats, luminescent jackets, and French berets with red neck scarves adorned by a pitch pipe attached to a spatula or long locks of hair. The girls sang in school choirs and musicals, churches, and for senior citizens and local organizations such as Aerospace America, the Office of Juvenile Affairs, and the Oklahoma Energy Resources Board. Their commitment to song— fostered by an SAI mission to harmonize the world—led to invitations to perform at a cultural exchange in Penang, Malaysia, and at a "Voices Down Under" Convention in Perth, Australia.

The talent of the three vocal majors and one piano major is nourished by their families, community, and school. Nancy Nortz, Tone Appétit coach and mother of tenor Katarina Nortz, describes the girls as positive role models. Honor roll students, the girls have interests that range from cross country to day care, student government to church, and reading to soccer. "The comment I get most often when I am with them at a performance or competitive event is not what great singers they are, but what wonderful people

Tone Appétit sings at a reception for quartets in Region 25 (Oklahoma, Texas, Missouri, Arkansas, and Louisiana). The girls competed against the best adult quartets in their region and finished ahead of half of them.

they are. Although they are always one of the youngest quartets at the Rising Star International Contest," said Nortz, "they have taken on a role of leadership and support for the other groups and have done a great deal to foster a sense of camaraderie and unity among the competitors."

"Singing is my passion," said Osburn, a vocal major who began singing publicly at age two. "You can express yourself in so many ways through music. The fact that Classen SAS offers so many different types of music classes really encourages me to learn as much as I possibly can about the art of music." In addition to studying piano and music theory, Osburn plans to play guitar and possibly drums.

Barbershop music, said Osburn, "can be beautifully soft or in-your-face loud. One of the great things about singing with other people is that you don't have to worry about making a fool of yourself. Rehearsals are great, too, because you don't just have to sit there alone practicing music over and over. We bounce ideas off each other, and we have lots of fun doing it. We usually end up spending about a third of our rehearsals laughing."

Part of the fun for Classen sophomore Emerald Lessley is the dimension her piano major offers her singing. "It adds a lot to my musical growth," she said, describing how playing what she sings helps her visualize what her voice is doing. "Playing the piano exposes me to a lot of music history," said Lessley, who added that understanding the composer's hard work gives her a greater appreciation of the music. "It's really awesome when we start to notice our sound getting better. When you have all the notes together it has this great sound, and when you do it right you get overtones—which absolutely rocks."

"Aside from being fun," she said, "[music] actually helps people with things like self-confidence, independence, self-expression, responsibility, individuality, and math skills." Through Young Women in Harmony, a youthful division of SAI for which she has acted as a recruiter, Lessley has

Joy in Barbershop Numbers

Barbershop began as an African-American art form in the early 1900s. Today this music is embraced by quartets and large choruses alike. Sweet Adelines International (SAI) has 30,000 members in more than 1,200 quartets and 600 choruses. Female members come from the United States, Australia, Canada, Japan, England, Finland, Germany, the Netherlands, New Zealand, Scotland, Sweden, and Wales. The Society for the Preservation and Encouragement of Barber Shop Quartet Singing in America (SPEBSQSA) is the world's largest all-male singing organization. It has 33,000 members in 800 chapters across the United States and Canada.

developed a network of friends around the world. "I now have friends in China, New Zealand, and Canada. It's a really cool thing."

Fourth-generation barbershop singer Katarina Nortz followed a family tradition. "I have been singing longer than I've been able to talk full sentences. It's my passion and what I love to do," said the 2003 Oklahoma Choral Directors Association (OCDA) Women's All-State participant who played "Ronny" in the musical *Hair*.

Lisa Marie Lopez advised would-be singers to give singing a try. "They may have stage fright, but when they get the guts to get up on stage and perform, it'll be more exhilarating than anything they've ever experienced. Words simply couldn't describe how much fun [barbershop] is," said Lopez, who played "Sheila" in the musical *Hair*. "A lot of little things combine to sing this style, things ranging from singing good vowels, breathing, voice placement, learning to sing confidently against three other voices, sight-singing, even emotional interpretation. In the end, no matter how much of your free time it has taken up or how many things you might have missed out on because of rehearsals, it's worth it when you're singing your heart out to an audience."

If you enjoying listening to music—if you sing in the shower or like to sing along to your favorite tunes—then joining a chorus or other vocal group may be for you.

2

Vocal Music

Music is part of our lives. We hear it on radio, CDs, television, and computers. We sing it in the shower, car, or at church. We go to concerts, stage productions, and movies. It can affect your mood, productivity, and health. If you enjoy singing, vocal music can be part of your school life.

VOICE

A wind instrument, the voice gets air from the lungs and vibrations in the larynx, or voice box. Using a muscle called the diaphragm that sits under the lungs, a singer forces air up from the lungs past vocal chords at the top of the windpipe. Vibrations cause sound, which is identified by three things—loudness or volume, its highness or lowness, called pitch, and a quality called tone.

Breathing, shape of mouth, and position of tongue affect the sound's volume and tone. The range of notes a voice can sing determines its place in a singing group. Soprano voices produce the highest sounds; bass voices are lowest.

From high to low, singers are grouped SATB: soprano, alto, tenor, and bass. Voices that fall in between those registers can be labeled soprano II or alto II, and opera singers fall into mezzo-soprano, contralto or countertenor, and baritone categories. Singers can pursue three basic singing styles: classical like opera and recital, popular like jazz and rock, and theater like show choir.

In the same way an athlete begins with a sport's basics and matures with practice, a choral singer starts with vocal basics and becomes more capable and accomplished over time. Choral directors introduce chorus members to exercises that condition the singing muscles. Sometimes singers have to retrain muscles to develop good habits for their

Students learn that music is exacting and takes practice. It can't be "almost right" or it won't sound good.

singing voices. Basic vowel sounds—EE, EH, AH, OH, OO—should be sung with a relaxed jaw, vertical mouth shape, and space inside the mouth to produce good tone.

COMMITMENT

Participating in choral activities requires time for lessons, rehearsals, class, independent practice, travel, and performance. Every member of a chorus contributes to its progress and success as a group.

Dr. Don Krudop, choral director at Salem High School in the Virginia Beach City School system and music teacher since 1975, ran five choirs in the 2003–04 school year. Krudop—who places students in groups based on vocal ability, level of commitment, and attitude—has room for anyone who wants to sing. "They come to learn that singing is easy, but that singing well is quite difficult," he said, equating the effort of scoring from zero to 95 in a competition the same as the hard work required to go from 95 to 98. "They learn that feeling emotion and passion is a good thing. They learn about the cultural significance of a universal art form in all its varieties and how music is an integral part of our daily lives," said Krudop, who added teamwork and discipline as additional benefits of chorus participation.

AUDITIONS

Choral auditions are common. Tryouts are especially necessary when the chorus has a limited number of openings and a need for specific kinds of voices. An audition can be private or public and involve singing solo, with others, and with prior preparation. Auditions can last five minutes or involve several short performances over a number of hours; they can be videotaped or recorded. Other students, parents, teachers, and administrators can be part of the team judging the auditions. It is important to know that not being chosen does not mean you have a poor voice. It can simply mean your voice does not fit the present needs of the chorus. In show choir auditions, for instance, the number of boys typically matches the number of girls to allow for partnered choreography. Non-singing criteria for this choral group include body build and dancing ability. First auditions are often followed by callbacks, a second chance to sing for a part.

Choral directors have different ways of running auditions. A student can be asked to sing a couple scales a capella or do some sight singing. Sight singing involves the ability to read music. Sometimes an instructor will teach the auditioning students a song to sing as part of their audition, but it is common for audition materials to be available ahead of time to allow students preparation time. Using a pitch pipe or hitting a piano key, a teacher can give students individual notes to test how they hear and match sounds. Typically, choral directors look for voices that blend and balance each other as well as singers who learn quickly and retain their parts. Singers have to exhibit accurate pitch and rhythm, a good vocal range and tone, and an ability to blend and project. Academic standing, motivation, organization, behavior, leadership, personality, and attitude are audition factors.

REHEARSALS

Once you've joined a chorus, you can expect more of what you sampled at your audition. Sessions start with warm-up exercises and scales. Starting with basic vowel sounds, you will work for unified sound and correct diction or pronunciation. You learn to follow hand and facial

The Curwen Hand Signs (major scale descending)

Choral directors use hand signs as a form of musical notation.

DO
fist, at forehead

TI
hand at eye level, pointer up

LA
relaxed hand hanging down
from wrist, at chin level

SOL
palm towards chest

FA
thumb down

MI
flat hand horizontal

RE
flat hand, palm down,
slanting upward

DO
The low "do" is the same as
the high "do," only the fist is
held at belt height

directions of the choral director and to achieve one choral sound through teamwork. Even when you are surrounded by voices singing other parts, you develop confidence in maintaining your own singing part.

The more you are involved with music, the clearer the messages you can send to your brain, which sends the how-to messages to your throat muscles. Singers learn relaxation techniques to keep those muscles from tightening up and affecting the sounds they produce. Gradually you will better understand how you sing, and learn to improve vocal resonance—how intense and prolonged your sound—by focusing tone behind the nose in an area called the mask. Under skilled supervision, you can increase your voice range. You will learn the difference between your chest voice and head voice, two different registers or voice ranges.

Good posture promotes good singing. When performing, you should stand up straight with feet apart. Hold your head up, keep your chin level, and focus your eyes on the choral director. Your hands should be at your sides and your shoulders comfortably relaxed. With mouth open wide, aim to reach the back of the room with your voice. As you become more skilled at reading music, you will identify the musical terms, symbols, and notes. Rehearsal drills will help you echo-sing and practice as a group.

Appointed or elected student officers can help run the choir. Students can manage apparel, set up and decorate for concerts, maintain the choral library, assist with handouts, help collect money, and raise funds.

PERFORMANCE

In addition to seasonal concerts at winter and spring, choirs can perform in contests and in the community, at shopping malls, service clubs, or nursing homes. Concert dress is required for performances. Uniform robes or black skirts/pants with white shirts are common; some choirs require tuxedos and uniform chorus dresses. Concert attire can be strict, prohibiting perfume or after-shave scents and limiting the types of earrings or shoes. Sometimes choirs wear clothes that fit a concert theme. Washington's Mount Baker eighth graders, for instance, once donned scientific lab coats for a rendition of "Monster Mash."

Besides performing as a large-group choir, many vocal students branch off into small ensembles for competition. Chamber ensembles, sextet, triple trio, octet, or quartet fit this category.

VALUE

Ruth Knoll directed chorus at Wisconsin's Hartford Union High School for forty years until her retirement in 1998. "In a world where there is so much hurry, heartache, and upheaval, the power of words and music creates an uplifting experience that feeds the soul and permits an emotional outlet not found in any other area of life," said Knoll. Singing, she said, is self-expression molded through teamwork into a beautiful finished product. According to Knoll, choral participation can create lifetime camaraderie and tap skills a singer can carry into retirement years.

"In music they learn to be sensitive human beings. Vocal music allows the student to see how poetry and music composition are woven together to create an expressive musical selection," said Knoll. "Vocal music transcends academic lines in the study of history and how all peoples have expressed themselves in their own cultures through music."

A mixed middle and high school chorus performs songs from The Sound of Music *before an outdoor audience. In mixed choruses, members are switched to different sections of the chorus as they age and their voices mature.*

3

Vocal Programs

Different ensembles sing different types of music, and performance opportunities range from solo to duet, trio, quartet, or full chorus experiences.

Flower Mound High School in Flower Mound, Texas, has seven choirs, four of which have male and female singers. Approximately forty freshmen and sophomores in Jaguar Singers focus on concert songs. Varsity Blues is the upperclassmen concert group. Forty female underclassmen form the treble choir or soprano voices known as Baby Blues. Girls who sing with one of the concert choirs can join Azure, the women's pop, jazz, and show choir that rehearses before school. The Wire is a similar group for boys. Shades of Blue is the varsity pop, jazz, and show choir group whose members also sing in FM Voices, the school's varsity choir of about sixty sophomores, juniors, and seniors.

No matter what kind of music you like, the doors of several vocal music programs are open for you if you are willing to work hard.

MIXED CHORUS

Choirs that include males and females with a wide range of sound are considered mixed chorus. Mixed choral groups generally sing concert music, so this group is called concert chorus, chamber choir, or festival choir. Many students begin mixed chorus in elementary school and continue through middle and high school, but you can join chorus when you are older. As voices mature, chorus members sing in different sections of the chorus. Choral members might also participate in instrumental music programs.

The Indianapolis Children's Choir has 17 choirs for more than 1,700 singers from 289 area schools. Any student at Connecticut's Ridgefield Academy is eligible for the Middle School Chorus. Joining this ensemble group does not require an audition or singing experience, and rehearsals run two to three times weekly. Students perform at school concerts and assemblies, community events, and music festivals.

Chorus members at Edward R. Martin Middle School in East Providence, Rhode Island, learn to read music and sing songs as different as classical, pop, Renaissance, and gospel. Seventh and eighth grade choruses have won gold medals at the Great East Choral Festival in West Springfield, Massachusetts. Teamwork is part of their success according to choral director Robert Rappa.

MADRIGAL

Renaissance songs and baroque music are the mainstay of madrigal ensembles. Songs for this group are typically sung a cappella in four to eight parts but may be accompanied by a lute. Madrigal songs, which first appeared in the fourteenth century, now include Italian, English, German, and French selections. Spain, the Netherlands, Denmark, and Poland have also produced madrigals. Madrigals are

Members of the Georgetown Visitation Madrigal Singers perform during School Night at the Washington D.C. Convention Center.

often set to short love poems and distinguished by word painting and contrasts in harmony and rhythm. Each line in a madrigal might have its own tune.

"The participation and enthusiasm for this group is great," said Brian Wand, who leads the twenty-six-member Madrigal Choir at Benet Academy in Lisle, Illinois. "These students like to challenge themselves so I am able to give them literature that many high school groups wouldn't attempt," he said, naming Des Pres, Gabrielli, and Palestrina.

Other madrigal groups, like the Madrigal Choir of Binghamton, New York, perform sacred and secular works from medieval and current times. On a scale of 1 to 6, madrigal singers in Alaska's Kenai Peninsula Borough School

A Madrigal Dinner

Singing lords and ladies make a lavish production at a madrigal dinner. Medieval costumes and song transport this event to Renaissance times. Brooke High School in Wellsburg, Ohio, involves about one hundred fifty students in the set-up of its Madrigal dinner. The students serve, decorate, entertain, and clean up at their annual feast. During the evening, the 24-member choir performs to a sellout crowd of over 200 guests who enjoy the three-hour extravaganza, complete with a medieval menu from wassail to pork and beef dishes.

District aim to sing at a 4 to 5 level of difficulty. In 2002, the twenty-two-member Johnstown, New York, High School Madrigal Choir performed at Carnegie Hall.

GOSPEL

Gospel singing reflects African-American spirituals developed from Southern Baptist and Pentecostal church music. Fast or slow, this music is full of spirit, a vitality suited for the 2004 Super Bowl Gospel Celebration in Houston, Texas. Gospel is a tradition that relies on three voice parts, though basses are added to sing spirituals. Students learning gospel often move while singing, clap the even beats, hum some parts, and incorporate piano and drums. Like jazz, gospel uses improvisation.

Founded in 1995, the International Gospel Music Hall of Fame and Museum in Detroit, Michigan, is dedicated to preserving this music worldwide. This organization dates gospel music from 1650 work songs and spirituals for which singers kept rhythm by clapping, playing homemade instruments, or clicking dry animal bones. Gospel Hall of Fame members include Mahalia Jackson (1997), Della

Reese (2001), and Dr. Dorothy Grant (2003). By 1996, gospel music recordings hit $538 million in sales, and the next year this music category grew by 32 percent—more than any other popular genre.

Eastern High School Choir in Washington D.C., is an internationally renowned choir that sings spirituals, blues, jazz, and contemporary gospel. Eastern twice placed first at the National High School Gospel Competition in New York City, and it has been recognized by the Kennedy Center for the Performing Arts.

South Carolina Congressman James E. Clyburn saw the Calhoun County High School Gospel Choir of St. Matthews, South Carolina, perform on Martin Luther King Day. "When I saw the Singin' Saints in January, I was so impressed with their power and poise that I decided that day to find a way to show off this choir in Washington," Clyburn said. He arranged for the group to remember September 11th with a performance at the Congressional Black Caucus Foundation's Annual Legislative Conference Gospel Extravaganza in Washington, D.C. Calling their performance extraordinarily moving, Clyburn said, "These young people represent the faith and hope of our nation as it is reflected in the faces of youth."

JAZZ CHOIR

Improvisation is the cornerstone of vocal jazz. Scat singing, a spontaneous utterance of nonsense syllables like bo-be-do-ba, is a standard jazz improvisational technique. Jazz charts, or pieces of music, give chord patterns but invite the singer to fill in the spaces. In jazz, scat carries meaning and enhances the song, even though the syllables themselves are meaningless. Scat singers sometimes imitate the sounds of trumpet, sax, drums, or piano.

Adaptations of instrumental sounds are called inflections. Creativity or the addition of new ideas and sounds is one way a competitive jazz choir is judged.

Jazz rhythm has a beat divided into thirds and the first note in a pattern of eighth notes is held longer than the second note. The accented beats in jazz are two and four. Tone quality in jazz is important and generally formed in the front of the mouth without vibrato or exaggeration. Some choral directors try to make singers project different moods by relating their exercises to colors. Singing a song in yellow, for instance, will sound cheerful while singing it in blue will be an expression of sadness. Singing in different colors helps students emphasize different tones.

During rehearsals, jazz singers sometimes face each other in a circle so they are aware of the group sound. Jazz choirs typically have 16 to 30 singers who, without any planned choreography, move during performance. Singers usually stand on risers and wear costumes. They use microphones and are accompanied by a rhythm band—piano, bass, and drums.

SWING CHOIR

Swing choir is a moderate version of the jazz choir. Performances center around popular songs and themes, but the costumed choreography is less involved than that of a show choir. The 16 to 30 members tend to be equally split between girls and boys. This group performs from different arrangements of risers and boxes and can be accompanied by piano, electric bass, drums, and wind instruments.

ALL-GIRL OR ALL-BOY GROUPS

The sound of an all-girl or all-boy choir is different from the sound of a mixed chorus. A merging of girls' voices is generally higher, and all-girl choirs are called treble choirs or glee clubs. Treble choir music can include pop, folk, and classical songs. Boys' voices differ in sound depending on age. Young boys have higher voices, and older boys produce deeper sounds. Some songs suitable for men's choir are "Yellow Submarine," "Love Potion No. 9," and "Workin' On The Railroad." Each set of voices has range, though, which makes girls' and boys' barbershop groups possible. Some men's choirs sing a certain style, like 1950s doo-wop songs. Five Colorado high school senior boys who formed an a cappella group called Out of Style performed "Come Go With Me" in 1998 for the purpose of one member asking a girl to the Homecoming dance.

Members of the Thomas More High School chorus in St. Francis, Wisconsin, rehearse while keeping their eyes on the choral director.

BARBERSHOP

Between 1939 and 1945, men and women discovered barbershop. These traditionally all-male or all-female groups sing a cappella in quartets or in larger multiples of four. "Sweet Georgia Brown," "Shine On Harvest Moon," and "Sixteen Tons" are among barbershop classics. Barbershop melody is sung by the lead voice below the tenor harmony. This music has a strong bass line and uses mostly major triads or three-note chords. Singing barbershop requires precision, energy, harmony, and good listening skills. The girls of Swing Low, one of two female barbershop quartets at Gaithersburg, Maryland's Quince Orchard High School, often sing through lunch for the fun of it.

SHOW CHOIR

Show choir is top entertainment with glitter, sequins, backdrops, props, lights, action, and singing. The number of males and females in show choir is usually equal to make dance numbers easier. Show choirs number from 16 to 60, and the back-up band can include electric piano, synthesizer, or computer directed sequencer track. Special lighting effects and costume changes can be part of a show choir routine. Energy is key to this thematic performing group that uses popular music, rock songs, and Broadway tunes.

MUSICALS

Beauty and the Beast, Peter Pan, Little Shop of Horrors, Phantom of the Opera, and *Charlie Brown* are musicals—performances with song, dance, and spoken words. Preparation for this type of performance involves weeks of rehearsals and memorization of speaking lines, lyrics, and choreography. Costumes, make-up, lighting, publicity, and set-building are part of the production. The experience of working on a musical is intense but relatively short-lived. A school usually produces only one musical per year.

Musical selection is based on many details. Choral directors consider the number of solo and choral singing parts and whether or not the script can be edited. Stage size, story length, how easily costumes can be obtained, how long it would take to make the scenery, and the number of costume changes are factors. Usually there is a rental fee for the use of the script, or dialogue, and the score, or music; the basic music often needs to be adapted for several orchestra parts. How well the musical suits the students and whether or not it has a worthwhile plot are key factors. Students who audition for musical parts are selected on the basis of singing skills and how well their personality fits the character they want to play.

OPERA

An opera is a serious, comic, or heroic story acted out on stage with libretto, the sung words. Operas include *Aida, Carmen,* and *Madame Butterfly*. A short opera with a light, humorous theme is called an operetta and has some spoken dialog. *The Mikado* and *Pirates of Penzance* are operettas. Operas began in 1637 in Italy but have been written in other languages like French, German, Russian, Czech, and English. An orchestra plays for an opera production that can include dancing and non-singing walk-on parts. If an opera is sung in an unfamiliar language, English translations are often projected above the stage or on audience seat backs.

Singing parts are written for the standard SATB parts, but opera also includes mezzo-soprano, countertenor, and baritone voice parts. Some operas include ballet dancing or a children's chorus. A chorus and individuals sing in an opera. Sometimes it's not clear whether a musical play is an opera or a musical. If all the words are sung, it is an opera; if there are also speaking parts, it might be an operetta or a musical. *Fiddler on the Roof, The Sound of Music,* and *Hansel and Gretel* could be presented in different formats.

Opera is not a typical cocurricular activity, but different opera companies visit schools around the country and perform to help students appreciate opera. The Utah Festival Opera Company will assist any opera-trained Utah teacher by lending specialists in writing, music, drama, and art. The company also offers a summer REACH program to about one hundred eighty students ages six to fourteen who write their own operas. Past original operas have been *The Adventures of Candyland, The Uno Opera, Robin in the Hood,* and *A Pokeman Opera.*

COMPETITION

Every type of vocal ensemble is eligible for competition. Contests are an opportunity to strive for personal growth,

Sound Collisions

While a hummingbird flaps its wings 50 times per second, human vocal chords, also known as folds, singing a middle C note collide 256 times in one second. For a three-minute song, soprano singers can have up to 90,000 collisions per second compared to about 40,000 collisions for a tenor or baritone. Entertainers who rehearse daily and perform regularly experience millions of collisions; avoiding swelling of folds or voice injury through proper care is critical. Singers should drink seven to ten eight-ounce glasses of water daily, warm up before performances, and rest their voices afterward.

compare ensembles, receive constructive criticism from an unbiased judge, and establish or continue a winning school tradition. For solo and ensemble contests, students have the opportunity to sign up for multiple contest categories. The preparation for solo, duet, trio, quartet, and ensemble contests is demanding. Each music category has specific details on which the singers are judged.

The Black Music Caucus of New York, a twenty-six-year-old organization, sponsors national school gospel choir competitions for elementary, middle, high school, and college choirs. More than a dozen awards honor categories such as outstanding female or male soloist, most musically coordinated dance ensemble, and most outstanding choral attire or accompaniment section. Middle and high school choir participants in USA Fest are categorized by enrollment numbers. A school must have at least six hundred students to send a choir to this festival, which is open to mixed concert choir, chamber or madrigal choir, and men's or women's groups. Some two hundred schools compete each year at Musicfest Orlando at Walt Disney World Resort. In addition to choral competition, there are Musicfest contests for concert bands and orchestras, jazz ensembles, marching bands, and auxiliary units like drill teams and flag-bearers.

It is important to choose an instrument you feel comfortable playing. Keep in mind that different instruments go with different types of music ensembles, such as concert band, marching band, or jazz band.

4

Instrumental Basics

Paul Spaeth, a student at the University of Southern California Thornton School of Music, began piano lessons at age five. Before he followed his dream to write music for films, he went to music camp, sang, played keyboard and bells, and recorded and sold his own CDs. "My band and choir directors throughout middle and high school have encouraged my musical development in ways I would have not been pushed otherwise," said Spaeth, recalling his Slinger, Wisconsin, school days and statewide honors prompted by a middle school band director who first showed him he could succeed. "I wrote pieces for my school band and choir and not only learned so much about the compositional process, but also gained invaluable perspective on the potential my music contained. I was moving people and affecting people through music," he said.

Participating in cocurricular instrumental music programs has rewards beyond the classroom. Instrumental music speaks a worldwide language. With practice, all band members can make music an enjoyable part of their lives.

THE ROOTS OF MUSIC

When music began is unknown, but we are surrounded by the sounds of nature—thunder, wind, raindrops, howling wolves, chirping birds, roosters, ocean waves. Sounds have meanings, and man has learned to imitate sounds for different purposes. Researchers think early man used music to communicate, honor, express feeling, or share group values. Instruments of music, such as conch shells, sticks, and voices, have long been with us. Ancient Sumerian carvings from 3000 B.C. show a procession of musicians. By 1600 A.D., European orchestras were performing. Today, one D.J. with the right equipment can approximate the sound of an entire orchestra.

INSTRUMENT FAMILIES

Instruments are grouped according to how they are made and how they sound. Stringed instruments are the violin, viola, cello, harp, and double bass. Woodwinds include the flute, piccolo, clarinet, bass clarinet, oboe, bassoon, double bassoon, and cor anglais. Brass instruments

Music in Everyday Objects

The entertainment troupe STOMP can turn a kitchen, laundry room, or simulated sewer into a musical extravaganza. Without any words, this creative cast can make music by simply jingling keys, stirring coffee, playing cards, or eating apples. In three weeks of performances, they use 30 sink plugs, 36 fifty-gallon oil drums, 120 kilos of sand, 84 brooms, and 72 pairs of drum sticks.

are the horns, trumpets, trombones, and tubas. Percussion instruments are the bass drum, timpani, triangle, side drum, xylophone, and gong. Other percussion instruments—castanets, sleigh bells, finger cymbals, wood block, wind machine, slapstick, and rain stick—can be added as needed for a particular performance. Keyboard instruments are piano, organ, and synthesizer. Different cultures also use native instruments to make music.

Deciding which instrument to play should start with a family discussion. Larger instruments require storage space; high-pitched or loud sounds will affect the entire household. Rental fees or purchase costs can also be a factor. Your school may have some instruments for student use,

The clarinet is one of the woodwind instruments. Clarinet players are seated together in the same section of the band, as are other players of the same instruments. This makes it possible for the conductor to signal to a particular instrument group.

and your local music store may offer discounted fees for students at schools with whom they do business. Consider whether or not you can transport your instrument on the school bus or if you will need someone to drive you back and forth to band practice. Schools can house the largest instruments, though students often have a similar instrument that remains at home for practice.

Comfort level and personal preference are important. A student who wears braces or has asthma will be drawn to some instruments more than others. School bands operate with a certain number of instruments, so open spaces help determine what players are needed. What sound you enjoy should help you make a decision. Follow a family tradition or try something entirely new: it is up to you.

Like any other tool, a musical instrument needs upkeep. Instruments need a thorough cleaning once a year and routine cleaning after each use. Cleaning cloths, brushes, polish, or oils are stocked at music stores. Some instruments, like the trombone, can be completely taken apart and washed in a bathtub. Complicated instruments like the flute should be cleaned annually by a professional. Certain instruments need occasional parts, like strings for a guitar or reeds for a saxophone. Carrying cases protect an instrument from harm and make transportation easier. Metronomes, tuners, and music stands are useful when you practice at home.

MUSIC LESSONS

Band members have group rehearsals and individual lessons. The purpose of a lesson is to make individual progress. Musicians prepare material before lesson time and benefit from one-on-one attention from the band director. Typical lessons include playing musical scales and songs.

International Music Day

October 1st in many countries marks Music Day, a celebration of creativity and heritage. International Music Day began in 1975 as a way for the International Music Council—a group sponsored by the United Nations Educational, Scientific, and Cultural Organization (UNESCO)—to help all children and adults enjoy the right to express themselves musically and listen, learn, and respect the music of different cultures.

Lesson attendance often counts as part of your band grade. Sometimes band directors will encourage students to seek private, regular lessons outside of school or suggest a summer music camp experience to maximize learning time. Lessons offer students an opportunity to clarify unclear directions or seek help on difficult music parts.

ADAPTABILITY

Different instruments lend themselves to different bands. Brass and reed instruments play jazz, and marching band demands easy-to-carry instruments. Occasionally students will play one instrument in the concert band and a different instrument in the marching band. It is possible to change the instrument you play, but it could mean learning music in a new way. Once you are used to playing a flute, for instance, switching to a saxophone may require a different way of breathing. If you think you might want to try several different instruments, talk to your band director. Some schools offer summer programs for the purpose of exposing musicians to new instruments. Your band director can also suggest what new instruments might be good for you based on what you have learned already and the kind of musician you are.

Percussion instruments include all types of drums as well as the triangle, xylophone, and gong.

FIRST CHAIR SELECTION

Musicians in a band are arranged in sections of similar instruments. Within each section a section leader is responsible for making sure the musicians in the group rehearse and know what the band director wants them to do. The seating arrangement in concert band or the standing arrangement in jazz band is determined by an order of excellence. The band director awards "first chair" to the most accomplished student in the section. Subsequent assignments follow in order. A section can be large with many chairs, and several musicians may share the same chair designation. In many music programs, musicians can challenge their seating placement by arranging for a kind of contest between themselves and those occupying the seat in question.

Band members are part of a group and have to uphold their part of that membership. By keeping up with their music lessons and rehearsals, musicians contribute their best to the sound of the band. Band members should eat a balanced diet, get the required amount of sleep, and keep up with their academic workload. In the event a marching band member is absent, for instance, there will be a hole in the lineup that no one else can fill. Musicians should keep their instruments, band uniforms, and music charts in good repair. Band members typically have to raise funds to travel and represent their school, community, and state well.

One type of instrumental ensemble is a drum corps. Drum corps is a competitive marching band composed of brass and percussion instruments as well as a color guard.

5

Instrumental Ensembles

Parade hits, salsa music, Broadway tunes, sports cheers, jazz improvisation, concert medleys, quiet solos, sectional songs–cocurricular bands have it all. Once you begin to refine your instrument-playing skills, you can judge what kind of music you most enjoy playing and which band is best for you.

MARCHING BAND

Marching band members are school ambassadors who represent their school in community parades, sports field shows, traveling clinics, performances, and competitions. Musicians typically begin to learn their music and marching steps in summer band camp before school starts. In some band programs, marchers receive physical education credit. Getting ready to march in a parade involves the entire group walking in step around the gym or a field or up and down town streets. Marchers usually wear matching school-color band uniforms that include hats, shoe covers called spats, and gloves. In cold weather states, marching band season is early fall and late spring. Marching band members double as orchestra members in the off-season. In mild-temperature states, marching band enjoys a longer season. Marching bands raise funds to cover travel expenses.

Marching band is part of a strong school band program. Georgia's Norcross High School Marching Band, comprising one hundred fifty students, has received many Grand Champion trophies in southern competitions. The school's Symphonic Band was named a 1996 Sudler Flag of Honor Band. The Sudler award from the John Philip Sousa Foundation recognizes bands that have exhibited high concert standards over a number of years. Graduating band members of the Norcross High School Band program were awarded over $1.5 million in college scholarships between 1999 and 2003.

The Waukesha, Wisconsin, North High School Band was named Wisconsin State Marching Band Champion in 1992, 1996, 1998, 2002, and 2003. Over the years, this band has played for President Ronald Reagan, Arizona's Fiesta Bowl Parade, the Washington, D.C. National Cherry Blossom Festival, and the Tournament of Roses Parade. Locally, the band performs for Special Olympics, the Salvation Army, and the Milwaukee Great Circus Parade.

ORCHESTRA

Large instrumental ensembles have different names depending on director choice and geographic location. Concert band, symphonic band, and orchestra are generally the same. Orchestra draws many musicians. The National Association of Youth Orchestras supports 125,000 young musicians in 1,800 youth orchestras and ensembles in the United Kingdom.

Marching bands move in formation as they play, and members must practice frequently in order to learn the steps and routines.

Mt. Ararat High School Concert Band musicians in Topsham, Maine, begin their training in elementary school. Belonging to a music ensemble exposes musicians to a variety of music and teamwork.

Alabama's Auburn High School Honors Band is one of only sixty-three high school bands worldwide to be placed by the John Philip Sousa Foundation on the Historic Roll of Honor of Distinguished Concert Bands in America, 1920 to Present. The same foundation awarded this band the Sudler Flag of Honor. Over the years, this Honors Band has placed more than seven hundred and fifty students in the Alabama All-State Band.

STROLLING STRINGS

Although they are generally seated in concert band, musicians who play stringed instruments can walk around to perform, too. Ineligible for jazz or marching band groups, the string section can form strolling ensembles, performing through the hallways of a senior center or from table to table at a dinner event, at civic or political functions or receptions. Strolling performances strengthen the public relations between school and community, and they help students develop pitch memory through memorization of music, better understand rhythm as they perform without a conductor, gain self-confidence and poise, and have fun providing community service.

Strings International Music Festival is an annual event in Philadelphia for one hundred seventy-five students who receive private lessons with a Philadelphia Orchestra member, ear training, and daily coaching at rehearsals. Anyone interested can join Washington's Bellingham High School Strolling Strings, who meet two mornings each week to learn new music. The United States Air Force Strolling Strings perform at the White House.

ENSEMBLES

Instrumental groups are called ensembles. Ensembles can be large or small, but ensemble most often refers to a small musical group of winds, brasses, or flutes. Part of the orchestra, ensembles can perfect their technique as a sectional group and concentrate on music made for their particular instruments. San Diego's Mt. Carmel Wind Ensemble I is under the direction of Warren Torns, who was honored in the late 1990s by the John Philip Sousa Foundation as one of America's top ten band directors. Mt. Carmel's Marching Sundevils appeared in a Snapple ad, performed in the Tournament of Roses and Fiesta Bowl Parades, and traveled to Austria, Canada, France, Germany, Great Britain, Japan, Hawaii, New York, and Switzerland.

"It is wonderful to see students from different cultures,

sometimes different languages interacting by playing music together," said Torns, who has been at Mt. Carmel since 1990 and a high school music teacher since 1970. "We firmly believe that you learn things by being in band, orchestra, or choir that will become a part of your life. The ability to set goals, to help others succeed, and be a part of a social, academic, and personal team that includes over two hundred people is an experience that is unique to being in band." Torns believes in placing students where they can succeed. Being a band member at a large school, he said, can make the transition to high school life easier. "We work to develop their potential as people through leadership training and by monitoring their growth as individuals, their potential as students by having high expectations, and their potential as musicians by presenting them with a multitude of options for performance."

JAZZ BAND

John Philip Sousa once said, "Jazz will endure just as long as people hear it through their feet instead of their brains." Jazz is foot-tapping music. An American art form, jazz covers traditional New Orleans style, Duke Ellington swing, Charlie Parker be-bop, Miles Davis cool jazz, John Coltrane free jazz, and Herbie Hancock fusion. When the performing ensemble known as Rhythm & Brass visited Wisconsin's Hartford Union High School musicians in December, 2003, trumpeter Rex Richardson told the group passion and commitment were keys to musical success.

Jazz is a personal musical opportunity to express feeling. "You let people in to hear a window of you," said Greg Keel, saxophonist and teacher at MacPhail Center for the Arts and Normandale College in Minneapolis. "The way you play on any given day expresses your feelings and emotions

Being part of a marching band means being part of a team, and members gain valuable experience learning how to work with a diverse group of individuals toward a common goal.

at that moment," said Keel, whose former students have played with the Temptations, Doc Severinson, Sting, Michael Jackson, and Stevie Wonder.

The logo for the Smithsonian Jazz Appreciation Month is "Live it, Learn it, Love it." Jazz at Lincoln Center runs over four hundred events each year, and its Essentially Ellington High School Jazz Band Competition and Festival attracts jazz bands from across the nation. Finalists are selected on the basis of improvisation, interpretation, soulfulness, technique, and tone. In its first eight years, the Jazz at Lincoln Center music education program distributed Duke Ellington music to over 186,000 high school musicians. The program also runs an essay contest in which high school musicians describe a personal jazz experience. Florida's Sarasota Jazz Society takes jazz history into the city's fifth grade American history classrooms. Howard Bankhead, executive director of the Tennessee Valley Jazz Society, has taken jazz into K-8 classrooms for twenty-one years. Matching jazz to math, Bankhead tells students that anyone who can count can play music.

PEP BAND

Igniting school spirit is the goal of pep band. This group plays for sports functions like football or basketball games, soccer matches, or pep rallies. Some pep bands accompany their school sports teams on the road, especially to major competitions like state title games. Pep band can be a volunteer activity for which band uniforms are not always required.

PIT BAND

Musicals require music provided by a pit band. This band is usually not visible, but the music it plays is critical to the stage production. Instruments depend on the musical being performed. Pit bands generally rehearse after school and perform when the musical hits the stage.

SOLO AND ENSEMBLE

After the in-school contest for chair placement is decided, the band plays as a unit and has many competition opportunities. Regional solo and ensemble contests are common. Once a year, one area school will host a Saturday marathon of contests that are judged by adjudicators—guest music teachers and professionals with judging experience. Students can choose the events in which they wish to compete. Multiple entries are not unusual, and one student

Musicians may form an ensemble to focus on music written for their type of instrument.

may perform in solo, duet, small ensemble, and large group contests. Judges score contestants on their competence, poise, and mastery. Top winners in this contest advance to state competition. Students win medals at both levels and can maintain or enhance the band's reputation through their efforts.

BAND BEYOND SCHOOL

Students who wish to pursue their music beyond the rigors of school rehearsals, lessons, performances, and competitions can take private lessons. Many students attend a summer band camp to receive top-notch instruction and work with musicians from other schools. Indianhead Arts and Education Center (IAEC) in Shell Lake, Wisconsin opened in 1968 and claims to be the longest continuous-running summer jazz camp in the country. Open to students in grades seven to twelve, the University of Wisconsin-supported IAEC summer music camps support jazz musicians, concert bands, and show choirs. Michigan's Interlochen Center for the Arts had a 2003 summer enrollment of over 2,000 students from 50 states and 37 countries. The oldest fine arts camp in the world, Interlochen offers junior high and high school students a variety of music ensembles—symphony orchestra, concert band, concert choir, operetta, jazz band, and string orchestra. California's Monterey Jazz Festival Summer Jazz Camp serves over one hundred fifty Monterey County student musicians. In 2003, its eleventh year, the festival launched a Summer of Jazz program that featured a U.S. and Canadian performance tour for the Monterey County Honor Band and a similar tour of Japan for the Festival's High School All-Star Big Band.

Hershey's All-USA High School Band

Dream, Reach, Succeed—the advertising campaign for Hershey's Fund Raising—was the casting call for a national recognition of outstanding high school musicians. Sponsored by Hershey Foods, Inc. and the National Association for Music Education, the Hershey's All-USA Band program solicited nominations from teachers, administrators, and private instructors. The All-USA Band, which was unveiled in the fall of 2004, is composed of students who not only show musical devotion and talent, but who balance their commitments to family, community, school, and selves.

CONTESTS AND SCHOLARSHIPS

State, regional, and national contests are educational and exciting performing opportunities open to school bands. The Seattle Young Artists Music Festival Association holds an annual six-day festival for more than seven hundred young musicians from the United States and Canada. The contest is open to piano, string, woodwind, and brass players in grades five through twelve. The Southeast Iowa Band Masters Association (SEIBA) holds a high school concert band festival for Iowa bands. The U.S. Scholastic Band Association (USSBA), a Youth Education in the Arts (YEA!) program, has more than 400 member high school marching bands who are eligible for over 100 festivals plus regional and USSBA championships. Competition is based on eighteen classifications determined by school enrollment numbers. Every aspect of performance is evaluated in band competition: music choice, sound, interpretation,

Members of the Taipei American School Tri-M chapter, located in Taipei, Taiwan, perform at Jeou Mei Elementary School. In addition to performing, the chapter donated instruments, music stands, and method books, as well as providing beginning instruction for third through sixth graders at the school in the spring of 2004.

general and visual effect, creativity, rhythm, and the band's stage presence.

Some schools offer band camp scholarships to a few deserving musicians each year. High school marching bands who participate in the Miss America Parade are eligible for scholarships up to $5,000. Winning schools determine which students will receive the award money.

At first, learning to play an instrument may seem like hard work, but the skills you learn by making a commitment to your music will help prepare you for other challenges in school, work, and life.

6

Musical Rewards

According to trombonist David Pavolka, who retired after thirty years as Director of Bands at Batchelor Middle School in Bloomington, Indiana, "In music, there is no bench. Everyone in the performing unit is a starter and as such shares the responsibility equally for the success or failure of the unit. By participating in a music program, each student is actively and directly employing principles of math, science, language, social studies, [and] history."

"Some of the best things about music participation for kids are not necessarily academic," said Pavolka, who has traveled to forty states for concerts, clinics, and judging assignments. "The . . . social aspects, being part of a team, doing something positive and creative with your peers and adults, the 'magic' of music performance are all important."

TEAMWORK

Most middle and high school classes last for a semester or two, but band continues from one year to the next, building tradition and camaraderie among its members. If you remain in the music ensemble you joined in sixth grade, you will have seven years of musical experience, friendships, memories, and achievement by the time you graduate from high school.

Sixth-grade Texas students in the Plano School District must participate in band, choir, or orchestra. These required classes meet daily, and the independent district runs twenty orchestra programs among its middle and high schools. Thirty years ago, the number of music students in the program was fifty. In 2004, there were 2,950 music students. Similarly, the string program that began as an after-school activity in 1974 with 50 students now attracts 2,952. The Plano musicians periodically stage cluster concerts in the high school gym for about eight hundred performers at a time, and the district has built a winning tradition. For seven years Plano has produced the Texas Honor String Orchestra, and in 2003 the Plano East Senior High School Chamber Orchestra was named Texas High School Honor Orchestra. The Plano Senior High School Symphony Orchestra, second runner-up in the Full Orchestra Honor Orchestra Competition, performed at the 2003 Midwest International Band and Orchestra Clinic by invitation. Nearly 100 percent of Plano students go on to college with about 15 percent pursuing music majors. The goal of the program, though, is a lifelong appreciation of music.

COMMUNITY STEWARDS

Traditionally, local school bands provide Christmas concerts, play at football games, march in parades, and send off the most recent graduates. Schools depend on their bands to represent them at community events and competitions, provide music for their theater productions, and spark the spirit of students assembled at a pep rally. Though the yearly events are routine, the band is constantly evolving with incoming and graduating members. Over the years, the band accumulates a record of accomplishment that each new group hopes to maintain, if not better. Veteran band members are role models for the newest members, and the band director oversees them all.

When Wisconsin's Slinger High School Marching Band needed new uniforms in 1997, the community stepped up to help. Band parents helped raise $45,000 for the 200 band and 30 auxiliary guard uniforms that cost $345 apiece at the time. The local school board paid the rest. When the same band had an opportunity to march in the 2001 Presidential Inaugural Parade, it raised $95,000 in seventeen days. David Hanke, twenty-eight-year band director, recognizes the special bond between band and community. "The people in this town take great pride in

Award-Winning Musicians

Some young people discover at an early age that music is their talent. Chad Lefkowitz-Brown, of Horseheads, New York, won the 2003 Junior High Instrumental Solo in the jazz and blues/pop/rock categories of *Down Beat Magazine's* twenty-sixth annual Student Music Awards. He had the opportunity to play alto sax with eighty-year-old drummer and jazz legend George Reed. Sixth grader Natasha Sinha, who started playing piano at age five, is the youngest composer to win the Morton Gould Young Composers Award—a competition for people under age thirty. Fifteen-year-old Sebastian Chang, who began piano lessons when he was four, was the New York Art Ensemble 2004 Young Composer Winner. Sinha and Chang were also among the 2001–2002 national winners in the Music Teachers National Association student competitions.

Playing a musical instrument may contribute to success in later life. In 1987, researchers interviewed over 1,000 congressmen and CEOs of Fortune 500 companies and found that over 90 percent had played a musical instrument in their youth.

their band and treat the members as if they are their own kids," he said. "It is a relationship that we will continue to nurture, and it is one in which we take great pride."

LIFE INFLUENCE

Music is often tied to patriotism. All major sporting events open with the singing of the National Anthem. Every branch of military service has its own band. Instrument associations, like the National Flute Association, International Double Reed Society, and North American Saxophone Alliance, encourage ongoing promotion of all types of musicians. Once you tap your musical ability, you join a worldwide family that speaks an international language.

Participating in school music programs influences some students to study music in college and pursue a teaching, composition, or performance career. Regardless of career choice, though, musical background leaves an imprint. The organizational and commitment skills, responsibility, and respect you learn as part of a singing or instrumental group make you a better team player in school, at work, and in life. Through exposure to different types of music, you better appreciate other sounds, rhythms, and cultures.

PERSONAL SUCCESS

Researchers make a convincing link between music and success. Studying music enhances students' listening and memory skills, helps them communicate across cultures, and teaches them the value of cooperative work. Musicians develop imagination, social poise, and self-esteem. Statistically, skilled musicians stimulate brain growth by as much as 25 percent in some areas, and music students out-perform their non-arts peers in the verbal and math parts of college entrance tests.

Composer and performer Isaac Hayes has been quoted as saying, "Have you ever wondered why young people take to music like fish to water? Maybe it's because music is fun. Plain and simple. It opens up their minds to dream great dreams about where they can go and what they can do when they get older." Former President John F. Kennedy once said, "The life of the arts . . . is close to the center of a nation's purpose—and is a test of the quality of a nation's civilization."

Glossary

a cappella–without accompaniment.

adjudicator–judge.

call back–an invitation for a second audition.

diction–pronunciation of vowels and consonants.

dynamics–singing loudly or quietly; how a voice expresses song.

ensemble–a musical group.

fusion–a type of jazz that is a mixture of jazz and rock.

harmony–chords that support the melody.

inflection–adaptation of instrumental sound.

larynx–voice box.

mask–an area behind the nose where singers focus musical tone.

melody–a succession or arrangement of musical notes.

overtone–an unsung musical tone heard above the highest tone of a balanced, matched chord.

pitch–how high or low a sound is.

pitch pipe–a handheld tool or set of pipes blown to set the pitch for singing or tuning an instrument.

projection–how a sound is sent out to the listener.

register–voice range.

resonance–the deep, full, reverberating quality of sound.

rhythm–beat.

score–music for a musical group.

tone–quality of sound.

treble–soprano, or high, voice.

vibrato–a rapid fluctuation of pitch for expressive and dynamic effect.

volume–how loud or soft a sound is.

Internet Resources

www.classical.net
Descriptions of classical music from medieval to modern times, reviews of over 2,800 classical CDs, and 4,000 links to other classical music Web sites.

www.ensemble.org
A collection of school music information including interesting music facts and links to state music organizations.

www.gospelchoirs.com/Competitions.htm
An international listing of gospel choir competitions.

www.highschool-acappella.com/groupindex.html
Regional listing of high school a cappella singing groups.

www.jazzatlincolncenter.org
Details programs and competitions at the nonprofit arts organization Jazz at Lincoln Center.

www.sbomagazine.com/howtobuy/sample.html
School Band and Orchestra Magazine gives tips for how to buy and repair instruments.

www.spebsqsa.org/web
The Society for the Preservation and Encouragement of Barber Shop Quartet Singing in America offers tips on how to sing in tune and how to be a great baritone, bass, lead, or tenor.

www.sweetadelineintl.org
Sweet Adeline International offers the definition, criteria, history, and competition information for women's barbershop.

www.swingmusic.net
Provides a history of jazz and audio archives.

Further Reading

Ardley, Neil. *A Young Person's Guide to Music.* New York: Dorling Kindersley Publishing, Inc., 1995.

Barber, Nicola. *Music, An A-Z Guide.* New York: Franklin Watts, 2001.

Danes, Emma. *Music Theory for Beginners.* London, England: Usborne Publishing Ltd., 1996.

Garty, Judy. *Techniques of Marching Bands.* Philadelphia: Mason Crest Publishers, 2003.

Klein, Joseph. *Singing Technique.* Tustin, California: National Music Publishers, 1972.

Marsalis, Wynton. *Marsalis on Music.* New York: W.W. Norton & Company, 1995.

Probasco, Jim. *A Parent's Guide to Band and Orchestra.* White Hall, Virginia: Betterway Publications, Inc., 1991.

Ryan, Pam Munoz. *When Marian Sang, The True Recital of Marian Anderson.* Singapore: Scholastic, 2002.

Shipton, Alyn. *Singing (Exploring Music).* Austin, Texas: Steck-Vaughn Co., 1994.

Tatchell, Judy. *Understanding Music.* London, England: Usborne Publishing, Ltd., 1992.

Thomas, Roger. *Groups, Bands & Orchestras (Soundbites).* Chicago, Illinois: Reed Educational & Professional Publishing, 2002.

Index

PICTURE CREDITS

Cover: Benjamin Stewart, Viola Ruelke Gommer, PhotoDisc.
Interior: ©Oscar C. Williams: 2, 14, 16, 22, 34, 37, 40, 45, 48, 50, 54; ©E.R. Lilley Photography: 8, 11; Courtesy of Erin Stewart: 19; P.R. News Foto/Sallie Mae Fund: 25; ©Ron Walloch Photography: 29, 42, 58; Courtesy of the Tri-M Music Honor Society: 52.

ABOUT THE AUTHOR

Judy Garty often writes with music playing in the background. She learned piano in elementary school and enjoys bands, parades, and concerts of all kinds. Besides writing another book for this series called *School Publications: Adventures in Media,* she contributed to two regional Wisconsin history books and to *Chicken Soup for the Kid's Soul.* Her other children's books include *Jeff Bezos: Business Genius of Amazon.com, Marching Band Competition, Techniques of Marching Bands,* and a biography on President Gerald Ford. Mrs. Garty especially likes outdoor jazz concerts and filling her house with jazz music or John Philip Sousa marching band songs.

SERIES CONSULTANT

Series Consultant Sharon L. Ransom is Chief Officer of the Office of Standards-Based Instruction for Chicago Public Schools and Lecturer at the University of Illinois at Chicago. She is the founding director of the Achieving High Standards Project: a Standards-Based Comprehensive School Reform project at the University of Illinois at Chicago, and she is the former director of the Partnership READ Project: a Standards Based Change Process. Her work has included school reform issues that center on literacy instruction, as well as developing standards-based curriculum and assessments, improving school leadership, and promoting school, parent, and community partnerships. In 1999, she received the Martin Luther King Outstanding Educator's Award.